Dedication

To my loving mother, whose faith and support have been my foundation.

To the Christian authors and publishers I have met through the years who have inspired me to leave my comfort zone and do what I thought I couldn't do.

And to all the readers, may this study deepen your understanding and bring you closer to God.

Table of Contents

Preface

As Father's Day approached, I felt a familiar heartache. Yes, I have an earthly father, and as of this writing, my parents have been married for sixty-six years. Yet, growing up, my dad was hardly around. He was a traveling salesman, home on weekends—sometimes every other weekend. When he was around, he would double down on what he thought a father should be: demanding and often punishing. Occasionally, there was physical abuse. My oldest brother bore the brunt of it, and I had my share as a teenager. My other siblings—two older sisters and a younger brother—were spared. My mom, though never physically abused, suffered in other ways, enduring a husband who was a functioning alcoholic, emotionally distant, and self-absorbed. It took a toll on her.

When my dad retired early, it was a shock to all of us re. He didn't know us, and we didn't know him. As a traveling salesman, he only knew what Mom told him, and she had spared him much of what was happening. Now, he was home, and I was making grown-up decisions that he didn't like. Though he wouldn't express his dislike to me directly, he would come down on Mom, blaming her for his perceived failures as a parent. In truth, she was, and is, both my mother and father, doing her best on her own.

Now, at 91, he has dementia. He doesn't remember some of what happened when I was growing up, or if he does, it's a version rewritten by his diseased brain. I've forgiven him for things I would never remind him of. I love him because he is my father, but I can't help but regret not having a dad who protected me, taught me things, gave fatherly advice, met my boyfriends, and told me he loved me without prompting.

When I visit my parents, I stop by his room, hug him, and tell him I love him. It's hard, but I do it. He is not the man he once was; whether that's better or worse, I don't know. He is frail, a mere shell of his former self. I doubt I will ever get an apology, but that's okay. Despite him still being earthbound, I grieve him. In doing so, I have felt the need to explore the aspect of God as my Father, to dwell on His fatherly attributes, and to know Him as a Dad. Whatever I lacked from my earthly father, I have found in God, my Father.

In a world filled with uncertainty and turmoil, the nurturing love of God our Father stands as a beacon of hope and comfort. Join me as we explore the aspects of God's nurturing love; he is our comforter, provider, protector, healer, and guide.

Your sister in Christ,

Hope

INTRODUCTION:

Welcome to "Embracing Our Father's Love: A Journey of Faith and Healing." This Bible study invites you to delve deeper into the heart of God and discover His abundant love, provision, protection, healing, and patience as our Father. This study is not just for those who have had an absent father, but for everyone. It is designed to guide you through a transformative exploration of Scripture, helping you cultivate a richer, more personal relationship with your Heavenly Father.

What You Will Discover:

Throughout this study, we will explore the many facets of God's love and care for us. Each chapter will provide insights into God's nature, revealing how He comforts us in our sorrows, provides for our needs, protects us in times of danger, heals our wounds, and patiently guides us through life's trials. He is so much more than what an earthly father should be. These nurturing aspects of God's character are profoundly relevant and impactful for your daily life.

How This Study Works:

• *Scripture-Focused Insights:* Each chapter is anchored in Scripture, offering a foundation of truth to build upon. Key passages will illuminate God's character and promises, providing a source of strength and encouragement.

• *In-Depth Bible Stories:* We will revisit familiar Bible stories with a fresh perspective, delving into the details to understand how God's love and power were manifested in the lives of His people. These stories will serve as powerful examples of God's faithfulness and compassion.

• *Practical Applications:* Along with theological reflections, you will find practical applications designed to help you integrate biblical principles into your daily routine. These applications are crafted to be relevant and actionable, bridging Scripture and everyday life.

• *Personal Prayers:* Each chapter includes a prayer to help you connect with God personally. These prayers open your heart to His presence and deepen your spiritual journey.

• *Reflective Questions:* At the end of each chapter, you will find questions that encourage further reflection and application. These questions will help you engage deeply with the content and consider how it applies to your life.

• *Journaling Prompts:* To foster personal reflection and growth, each chapter offers prompts inviting you to explore your thoughts and experiences. Writing can be a powerful tool for internalizing the lessons and recognizing God's work in your life.

How to Use This Study:

This study is designed for flexibility, making it suitable for both individual and group use. You can work through it at your own pace, reflect on the questions and journaling prompts, or share the journey with others in a group setting. Each chapter builds on the previous one, but feel free to start with the topics that resonate most with you.

What you need:

- A pencil or pen.

- Coloring pencils or crayons

- Though space is provided for your answers, you may want a notebook or journal to answer your Bible study questions and for journaling.

- A Bible, you may want to follow along with your own Bible and make notes and highlight as you go along.

A Personal Invitation:

As you embark on this journey of faith and healing, I invite you to open your heart to the transformative power of God's love. Whether you seek comfort, guidance, healing, or a deeper relationship with your Heavenly Father, this study is meant to be a source of encouragement and renewal. Whatever relationship you have with your earthly father, know that God is our true Father. One who will never leave our side. May you encounter God's love in profound ways and experience the peace, strength, and joy from walking closely with Him.

> Heavenly Father, we thank You for Your unwavering love and faithfulness. As we begin exploring Your Word and deepening our faith, we ask for Your guidance and presence. Open our hearts to receive Your truths and help us apply them in our lives. May this study be a time of growth, healing, and transformation. In Jesus' name, Amen.

Chapter 1: God as Our Comforter

Introduction:

Finding comfort in the arms of our loving Father brings profound peace, even in the depths of our struggles. This chapter explores how God, as revealed in the Scriptures, provides comfort and how we can seek solace in His presence during challenging times. God's comfort is like a gentle embrace that envelops us, offering safety and love. Recognizing this divine comfort can strengthen our resolve to persevere through life's difficulties.

> **Genesis 16:13 (CSB):** "So she named the Lord who spoke to her: 'You are El-roi,' for she said, 'In this place have I actually seen the one who sees me?"
>
> **Psalm 34:18 (CSB):** "The Lord is near the brokenhearted; he saves those crushed in spirit."
>
> **Isaiah 41:10 (CSB):** "Do not fear, for I am with you; do not be afraid, for I am your God. I will strengthen you; I will help you; I will hold on to you with my righteous right hand."

Discussion:

God's comfort is as vital today as it was in biblical times. In moments of sorrow, loss, or anxiety, the assurance of His comforting presence provides profound relief. For example, when someone loses a job and feels abandoned, praying to God and reflecting on His promises can instill a sense of peace and hope. This divine comfort helps us trust that better days are ahead.

Practical Applications:

- Turn to the Bible and prayer when you feel low.
- Seek God's peace and comfort in your daily life.
- Share your struggles with members of your faith community for mutual support.

Bible Story: Hagar in the Wilderness (Genesis 16 and 21):

Hagar was an Egyptian maidservant to Sarah, Abraham's wife. Because Sarah was barren and desperate to provide an heir for Abraham, she suggested that Abraham have a child with Hagar. However, once Hagar became pregnant, she began to despise Sarah. This shift in Hagar's attitude caused Sarah to feel disrespected and threatened, leading to tension between the two women.

Sarah's displeasure grew, and she treated Hagar harshly. Unable to bear the mistreatment, Hagar fled into the wilderness. There, an angel of the Lord found her by a spring and instructed her to return to Sarah, promising that her descendants would be too numerous to count. Hagar called the Lord who spoke to her "El Roi," meaning "the God who sees me," acknowledging God's awareness of her suffering. She returned and bore Ishmael, living under Sarah and Abraham's care for many years.

Imagine Hagar's fear and loneliness in the wilderness. She was pregnant, cast out by those she served, and faced an uncertain future. Yet God's messenger found her and offered comfort and hope. This story reassures us that God sees our pain and cares for us deeply. God provides comfort and guidance, as He did for Hagar, no matter our circumstances.

Heavenly Father, I come before You seeking Your divine comfort. In moments of sorrow and hardship, help me to feel Your comforting presence and find peace in Your promises. Lord, guide me to embrace Your love and share it with others who are hurting. Amen.

Key Takeaways:

• God is always near to comfort us in times of trouble.
• Scriptures like Psalm 34:18 and Isaiah 41:10 affirm God's promise to heal the brokenhearted.
• Sharing our struggles within our faith community provides additional comfort and support.

Bible Study Questions:

1. How does Psalm 34:18 illustrate God's presence during challenging times?

_____

_____

_____

_____

_____

2. How can we experience God's comfort in our everyday lives?

_____

_____

_____

_____

3. What does the story of Hagar in Genesis reveal about God's comforting presence?

_____

_____

_____

_____

4. Why is it significant that Hagar calls God "El-Roi"?

_____

_____

_____

_____

5. How can we extend God's comfort to those in need?

_____

_____

_____

_____

I will not leave you comfortless: I will come to you.

John 14:18 kjv

Journaling Prompts:

1. Reflect on when you felt God's comfort in a difficult situation. How did it change your perspective?

_____

_____

_____

_____

_____

_____

_____

_____

_____

_____

2. Write about an area of your life where you need God's comfort. How can you invite His presence into this situation?

_____

_____

_____

_____

_____

_____

_____

_____

_____

_____

_____

3. Describe a moment when you felt alone or sad. How did God's promises in the Bible bring you comfort?

_____

_____

_____

_____

_____

_____

_____

_____

_____

_____

4. Think of ways to remind yourself of God's comforting presence during stressful times.

_____

_____

_____

_____

_____

_____

_____

_____

_____

_____

_____

_____

5. Identify someone in your life who needs comfort. How can you be a source of God's love for them?

_____

_____

_____

_____

_____

_____

_____

_____

_____

_____

El-Roi : the God
who sees me

Matthew
6:26

Chapter 2: God as Our Provider

Introduction:

Our Heavenly Father provides for all our needs, both material and spiritual. This chapter explores how God cares for us and how we can trust in His provision. Recognizing God as our Provider helps alleviate our worries and reinforces our trust in His unwavering care. Just as He cares for the birds and flowers, He provides for us.

Discussion:

In contemporary life, God's provision remains crucial. It's not limited to material goods but also includes meeting our emotional and spiritual needs. For instance, God provides companionship and solace in loneliness or despair.

God's provision teaches us to rely on Him. We can trust that He will provide for us when faced with financial hardships or significant needs. An example is a family struggling to pay bills; they might pray and find God's provision through unexpected means like a friend's generosity or a new job opportunity.

Exodus 16:11-12 (CSB): "The Lord spoke to Moses: 'I have heard the complaints of the Israelites. Tell them: At twilight you will eat meat, and in the morning you will eat bread until you are full. Then you will know that I am the Lord your God."

Philippians 4:19 (CSB): "And my God will supply all your needs according to his riches in glory in Christ Jesus."

Matthew 6:26 (CSB): "Consider the birds of the sky: They don't sow or reap or gather into barns, yet your heavenly Father feeds them. Aren't you worth more than they?"

Practical Applications:

- Trust God to provide in financial or personal struggles.
- Be grateful for daily blessings and share them with others.

Bible Story: Feeding the 5000 (John 6:1-14):

A great crowd followed Jesus because they saw the miraculous signs He had performed. Seeing the large crowd approaching, Jesus asked Philip where they could buy bread to feed all these people. Philip replied that even eight months' wages would not be enough to buy each person a bite. Andrew, another disciple, mentioned a boy with five small barley loaves and two small fish, but he doubted they would be enough for so many people.

Jesus took the loaves, gave thanks, and distributed them to those seated as much as they wanted, and did the same with the fish. When everyone had enough to eat, Jesus told His disciples to gather the leftovers, which filled twelve baskets. This miracle demonstrated God's abundant provision, showing that even a little, when blessed by God, can become more than enough.

Imagine the scene: thousands of people seated on a hillside, hungry and waiting. Jesus took a meager offering of loaves and fish and miraculously provided for everyone, leaving abundant leftovers. This story teaches us to trust God's provision, knowing He can provide for our needs even when it seems impossible.

Key Takeaways:

Dear Lord, thank You for being our ultimate Provider. Help me to trust in Your provision and be content with what You give. Teach me to be generous with others, reflecting Your love and care. Amen.

- God provides for all our needs, often in unexpected ways.
- Reflecting on stories like the feeding of the 5000 strengthens our faith in God's provision.
- Gratitude for God's provision encourages us to share with others.

Bible Study Questions:

1. How does the story of manna (bread) in Exodus demonstrate God's provision?

_____

_____

_____

_____

2. What does Philippians 4:19 teach us about God's ability to supply our needs?

_____

_____

_____

_____

3. How does the feeding of the 5000 illustrate God's abundance?

_____

_____

_____

_____

4. How can we deepen our trust in God's provision?

_____

_____

_____

_____

5. How can we assist others through God's blessings?

_____

_____

_____

_____

Journaling Prompts:

1. Reflect on a time when God provided for you unexpectedly. How did it impact your faith?

_____

_____

_____

_____

_____

_____

_____

_____

_____

_____

_____

2. Write about a part of your life where you need God's provision. How can you trust Him to meet this need?

_____

_____

_____

_____

_____

_____

_____

_____

_____

_____

3. List three things you're grateful for today and how they show God's provision.

_____

_____

_____

_____

_____

_____

_____

_____

_____

_____

_____

4. Describe a time when you worried about your needs. How did God provide or bring you peace?

_____

_____

_____

_____

_____

_____

_____

_____

_____

_____

_____

5. Think of someone who needs provision. How can you be a source of support for them?

_____

_____

_____

_____

_____

_____

_____

_____

_____

_____

_____

And Abraham called the name of that place Jehovah jireh: as it is said to this day, in the mount of the Lord it shall be seen.

Genesis 22:14

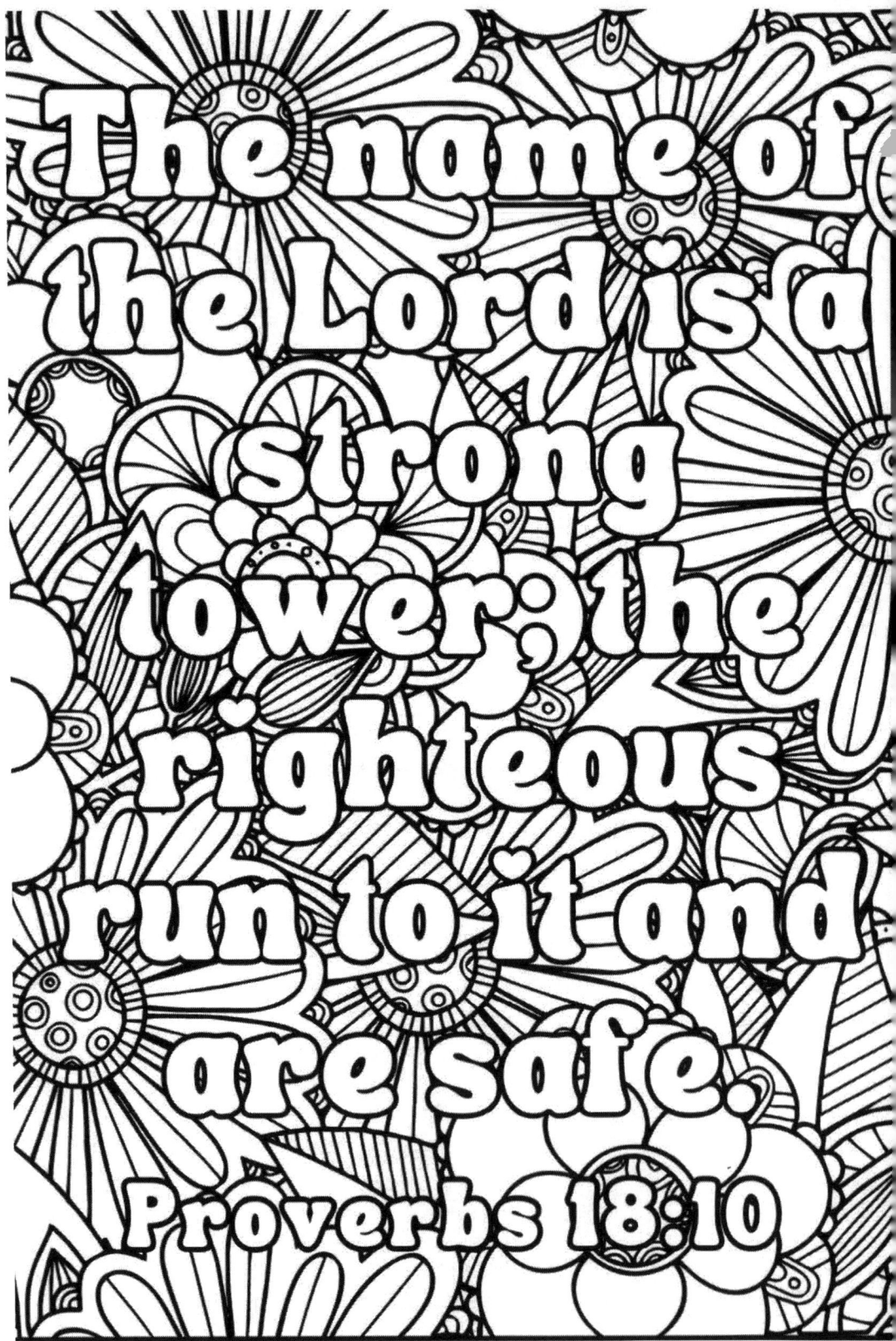

The name of the Lord is a strong tower; the righteous run to it and are safe.

Proverbs 18:10

Chapter 3: God as Our Protector

Introduction:

God promises to shield His children from harm and guide us through life's challenges. This chapter explores how God protects us and strengthens us during tough times. Knowing that God is our Protector instills a sense of security and peace, like having a robust shield guarding us from danger.

Discussion:

God's promise of protection offers peace and security in a world fraught with dangers and worries. His protection encompasses both physical and emotional safety, assuring him in the face of adversity.

God's protection signifies His constant presence, shielding us from harm and fortifying us for challenges. For instance, someone facing a health crisis might find comfort in knowing God is there, guiding them and providing strength. Even when unseen, God works tirelessly to protect and support us during difficult times.

> **2 Samuel 22:3-4 (CSB):** "My God, my rock, where I seek refuge, my shield, the horn of my salvation, my stronghold, my refuge, and my Savior—you save me from violence. I called to the Lord, who is worthy of praise, and I was saved from my enemies."
>
> **Psalm 121:7-8 (CSB):** "The Lord will protect you from all harm; he will protect your life. The Lord will protect your coming and going both now and forever."
>
> **Psalm 91:4 (CSB):** "He will cover you with his feathers; you will take refuge under his wings. His faithfulness will be a protective shield."

Practical Applications:

- Trust in God's protection through prayer during times of fear or anxiety.
- Recognize God's protective hand when dangers may not be immediately evident.

Bible Story: Daniel in the Lion's Den (Daniel 6:1-23):

Daniel was one of the top officials in Babylon, known for his faith and integrity. Some officials, jealous of his favor with the king, devised a plot to throw him into the lions' den. They tricked the king into issuing a decree that anyone who prayed to any god or man except the king within thirty days would be cast into the den of lions.

Despite the decree, Daniel continued praying to God three times a day. The officials reported him, and the king, though distressed, was compelled to follow the law and had Daniel thrown into the lions' den. The king hoped that Daniel's God would save him and spent the night fasting.

At dawn, the king rushed to the den and called out to Daniel. To his relief, Daniel replied that God had sent an angel to shut the lions' mouths, and he was unharmed. Overjoyed, the king ordered Daniel to be lifted out of the den and decreed that everyone in his kingdom should revere the God of Daniel.

Gracious Lord, I trust in Your protection and care. Guard me from harm and guide me through life's trials. Help me to rely on Your strength and find peace in Your promises. Amen.

Picture the fear and isolation Daniel must have felt, surrounded by lions in the dark den. Yet he trusted in God's protection, and God delivered him from harm. This story assures us that God's protective power is mighty and faithful, no matter the danger.

Key Takeaways:

- God's protection encompasses physical, emotional, and spiritual safety.
- Scriptures like Psalm 91 affirm God's promise of protection.
- Trusting in God's protection brings peace in times of fear and uncertainty.

Bible Study Questions:

1. What does David's song in 2 Samuel tell us about God's protective nature?

_____

_____

_____

_____

2. How does Psalm 91 describe God's care and protection?

_____

_____

_____

3. What lessons can we draw from Daniel's story about trusting God's protection?

_____

_____

_____

_____

4. How can we experience God's protection in our daily lives?

_____

_____

_____

_____

5. How can we help others recognize and trust in God's protective care?

_____

_____

_____

_____

Journaling Prompts:

1. Reflect on a time when you felt God's protection in a dangerous or stressful situation. How did it strengthen your faith?

_____

_____

_____

_____

_____

_____

_____

_____

_____

_____

_____

2. Write about an area in your life where you need God's protection. How can you seek His presence?

_____

_____

_____

_____

_____

_____

_____

_____

_____

_____

3. Describe a moment when you felt afraid or vulnerable. How did God's promises of protection bring you comfort?

_____

_____

_____

_____

_____

_____

_____

_____

_____

4. Identify someone who needs protection. How can you pray for and support them in trusting God?

_____

_____

_____

_____

_____

_____

_____

Daniel and the Lion's Den

```
R  A  S  E  A  L  D  F  D  A  R  I  U  S  I  I  E
E  O  V  E  R  S  E  E  I  N  G  A  G  T  I  N  E
G  N  I  M  H  I  N  N  O  C  E  N  T  C  I  M  A
T  I  K  E  U  C  L  S  L  T  H  R  I  V  E  A  D
A  H  M  P  L  I  O  N  S  S  A  T  R  A  P  S  U
C  E  A  D  M  I  N  I  S  T  R  A  T  O  R  S  K
C  D  X  E  N  P  I  C  I  I  O  I  L  L  E  A  I
U  A  I  C  O  P  L  N  S  H  A  E  R  R  B  S  N
S  L  N  D  E  N  M  V  T  D  A  N  I  E  L  T  G
A  A  T  E  M  L  R  T  O  E  N  L  H  G  V  S  D
T  J  E  J  P  O  L  L  N  G  R  T  S  M  C  G  O
I  D  G  C  E  R  U  E  E  T  L  C  H  A  R  M  M
O  E  R  S  U  A  A  T  N  A  Y  N  E  N  O  P  L
N  N  I  A  X  M  L  A  H  C  U  S  O  D  W  E  A
T  B  T  E  H  R  A  O  I  S  E  N  H  T  E  E  S
I  R  Y  D  T  P  R  N  U  D  T  S  M  M  R  D  I
E  D  P  E  R  S  I  A  N  S  O  A  D  I  O  R  O
```

Accusation	Administrators	Daniel
Darius	Den	Excellence
Harm	Innocent	Integrity
Interceded	Jealous	Kingdom
Lions	Mouths	Overseeing
Persian	Satraps	Seal
Stone	Thrive	

Solution on page 117

Jesus heals the blind man

Chapter 4: God as Our Healer

Introduction:

Healing is a profound expression of God's love. This chapter explores how God heals us physically, emotionally, and spiritually, illustrated through Bible stories and practical insights. God's healing power demonstrates His deep care for us. We can seek His healing for any ailment, whether physical sickness, emotional distress, or spiritual brokenness.

Discussion:

God's healing is significant in addressing our physical, emotional, and spiritual ailments. Many people testify to the power of faith and prayer in healing, demonstrating God's willingness to heal and restore.

God's healing is not limited to physical recovery but also includes emotional and mental restoration. For example, someone dealing with grief may find comfort and healing through prayer and Scripture. Trusting in God's healing power can uplift our spirits and provide hope for a brighter future.

Practical Applications:

- Seek God's healing in every aspect of your life.
- Trust in God's plan for healing, finding comfort in His Word.

> **James 5:14-15 (CSB)**: "Is anyone among you sick? He should call for the elders of the church, and they are to pray over him, anointing him with oil in the name of the Lord. The prayer of faith will save the sick person, and the Lord will raise him up; if he has committed sins, he will be forgiven."
>
> **Psalm 103:2-3 (CSB)**: "My soul, bless the Lord, and do not forget all his benefits. He forgives all your iniquity; he heals all your diseases."
>
> **Isaiah 53:5 (CSB)**: "But he was pierced because of our rebellion, crushed because of our iniquities; punishment for our peace was on him, and we are healed by his wounds."

Bible Story: The Healing of the Blind Man (John 9:1-12):

Jesus and His disciples encountered a man who had been blind from birth. The disciples asked whether the man's blindness was due to his own sin or his parents' sin. Jesus responded that neither was the cause; instead, it was an opportunity for God's works to be displayed in him.

Jesus then spat on the ground, made mud with the saliva, and applied it to the man's eyes. He instructed the man to wash in the Pool of Siloam. The man obeyed and, upon washing, returned with his sight restored. This miracle astonished his neighbors and those who had known him as a blind beggar, leading to questions about how he had gained his sight.

Imagine the joy and wonder the man must have felt, seeing for the first time after living in darkness. This story highlights Jesus' power to heal physical ailments and bring light and clarity to our lives. It assures us that no matter the affliction, Jesus has the power to heal and restore.

Loving Father, I come to You seeking healing in my body, mind, and spirit. May Your healing power restore and strengthen me. Help me to trust in Your goodness and share Your love with others. Amen.

Key Takeaways:

•	God's healing power addresses physical, emotional, and spiritual needs.
•	Stories like the healing of the blind man demonstrate God's ability to heal and renew.
•	Seeking God's healing through prayer and community support strengthens our faith.

Bible Study Questions:

1. What does James 5:14-15 teach us about seeking healing in a faith community?

_____

_____

_____

_____

2. How does Isaiah 53:5 reveal God's healing power?

_____

_____

_____

_____

3. What can we learn from the healing of the blind man about God's ability to heal?

_____

_____

_____

_____

4. How can we ask for God's healing in our lives?

_____

_____

_____

_____

5. How can we support others in their healing journeys?

_____

_____

_____

_____

Journaling Prompts:

1. Reflect on a time when you experienced God's healing. How did it impact your view of His power?

_____

_____

_____

_____

_____

_____

_____

_____

_____

_____

2. Write about an area in your life where you need healing. How can you invite God's healing touch?

_____

_____

_____

_____

_____

_____

_____

_____

_____

_____

_____

_____

3. Describe a moment when you felt broken or needed healing. How did God's promises bring you hope?

_____

_____

_____

_____

_____

_____

_____

_____

_____

_____

_____

4. List ways to seek God's healing daily. How can you invite His healing presence?

_____

_____

_____

_____

_____

_____

_____

_____

_____

_____

5. Think of someone who needs healing. How can you pray for and support them?

_____

_____

_____

_____

_____

_____

_____

_____

The Story of Jesus and the Blind Man

```
B S T P R E S A B B A T H S N P
S F A I T H M I R A C L E R E N
I G E S H W E S O T L C H C R S
N E L P A R E N T S E O T T E O
T E S T I M O N Y I H M H L B D
D H P T H D Y D N G A E P O I B
E G H A P A S N T H T I E L I L
E N A E O Z M I T T C D E E E I
J I R O D E D D B S A J M H E N
H H I T D U I A I E R E D P A D
E O S T M N G D P Y T S O S P S
A R E W A S H E O E E U U T N N
L L E H S I N G O S L S B C A L
I D S T G M N F L X S E T T O D
N O I G E H A N E I G H B O R S
G X B I U A E N B B O S T H L O
```

Solution page 117

Blind	Disciples	Doubt
Eyes	Faith	Healing
Jesus	Man	Miracle
Mud	Neighbors	Parents
Pharisees	Pool	Sabbath
Sight	Sin	Temple
Testimony	Wash	

MORE ✝ faith LESS·FEAR

God is our Loving Father

Chapter 5: God as Our Loving Father

Introduction:

God's love is profound and nurturing, embodying forgiveness, acceptance, and unwavering commitment. This chapter explores the depth of God's fatherly love, helping us feel secure and valued. Just like a loving father, God cares for us, forgives us, and is always there for us.

Discussion:

God's fatherly love means He accepts us unconditionally, providing comfort and a sense of belonging. For instance, individuals who feel unloved can find worth and acceptance by knowing they are God's beloved children.

When we understand God as our Father, we recognize His unwavering love. Just as a good earthly father forgives and welcomes us back, God's love gives us the confidence to face challenges, knowing we are not alone.

Practical Applications:

- Embrace God's love by seeking His forgiveness and guidance.
- Reflect God's love in your relationships by being forgiving and supportive.

Bible Story: The Prodigal Son (Luke 15:11-32):

Jesus told the story of a man with two sons. The younger son asked for his share of the estate, which he squandered on wild living in a distant country. As a severe famine struck, he

Luke 15:11-32 (CSB): "He also said, 'A man had two sons. The younger of them said to his father, "Father, give me the share of the estate I have coming to me." So he distributed the assets to them. Not many days later, the younger son gathered together all he had and traveled to a distant country, where he squandered his estate in foolish living."

1 John 3:1 (CSB): "See what great love the Father has given us that we should be called God's children and we are! The reason the world does not know us is that it didn't know him."

Romans 8:15 (CSB): For you did not receive a spirit of slavery to fall back into fear. Instead, you received the Spirit of adoption, by whom we cry out, 'Abba, Father!'

found himself in dire need and took a job feeding pigs, a humiliating position. Desperate, he returned to his father, hoping to be accepted as a hired servant.

While he was still far off, his father saw him, filled with compassion, ran to him, and embraced him. He ordered his servants to bring his son the best robe, a ring, and sandals and prepare a feast to celebrate his return. The father's joy contrasted sharply with the elder brother's anger, who felt neglected despite his loyalty.

Imagine the younger son's shame and fear as he returned home, expecting to be reprimanded. Instead, he was met with unconditional love and celebration. This story illustrates God's readiness to forgive and His joyful welcome when we turn back to Him, no matter our past mistakes.

Dear Father, thank You for Your boundless love and forgiveness. Help me to embrace Your love and extend it to others. May Your love guide my actions and relationships. Amen.

Key Takeaways:

• Understanding God's fatherly love provides comfort and a sense of belonging.
• Verses like 1 John 3:1 remind us that we are God's children.
• Reflecting God's love in our relationships fosters deeper connections.

Bible Study Questions:

1. What does the story of the Prodigal Son teach us about God's love?

_____

_____

_____

_____

2. How does 1 John 3:1 help us understand our identity as God's children?

_____

_____

_____

_____

3. How can we feel God's love in our daily lives?

_____

_____

_____

_____

4. How can we demonstrate God's love to others?

_____

_____

_____

_____

5. What does Romans 8:15 tell us about being adopted into God's family?

_____

_____

_____

_____

Journaling Prompts:

1. Reflect on a time when you felt God's fatherly love. How did it change your relationship with Him?

_____

_____

_____

_____

_____

_____

_____

_____

_____

_____

2. Write about a part of your life where you must feel God's love. How can you invite His presence?

_____

_____

_____

_____

_____

_____

_____

_____

_____

_____

3. Describe a moment when you felt distant from God. How did understanding His love help you reconnect with Him?

_____

_____

_____

_____

_____

_____

_____

_____

_____

_____

4. List ways to show God's love to others. How can you reflect His love in your relationships?

_____

_____

_____

_____

_____

_____

_____

_____

_____

_____

5. Think of someone who needs to experience God's love. How can you help share that love with them?

_____

_____

_____

_____

_____

_____

_____

_____

How can you help share that love with them?

_____

_____

_____

_____

Chapter 6: Embracing God's Nurturing Love in Daily Life

Introduction:

Living out God's love involves manifesting it in our daily actions and relationships. This chapter offers practical ways to embody God's love and care daily. Demonstrating God's love improves the world around us by showing kindness to someone at school or helping a neighbor in need.

Discussion:

Embracing God's love daily means demonstrating it through your actions and relationships. Kindness and patience improve the world, such as being kind to a stranger or assisting a friend in need.

When we act with kindness and patience, we reflect God's love to others. Simple gestures like kindness to someone on a bad day can profoundly impact those around us, showcasing God's love.

> ***Romans 12:2 (CSB):*** "Do not be conformed to this age, but be transformed by the renewing of your mind, so that you may discern what is the good, pleasing, and perfect will of God."
>
> ***Colossians 3:12 (CSB):*** "Therefore, as God's chosen ones, holy and dearly loved, put on compassion, kindness, humility, gentleness, and patience."
>
> ***1 Peter 5:7 (CSB):*** "Casting all your cares on him because he cares about you."

Practical Applications:

- Reflect God's love in your daily actions by showing kindness and forgiveness.
- Focus on God's love to respond with patience and understanding in challenging situations.

Bible Story: The Good Samaritan (Luke 10:25-37):

A man traveling from Jerusalem to Jericho was attacked by robbers, stripped of his clothes, beaten, and left half-dead. A priest happened to go down the same road, but when he saw the man, he passed by on the other side. Likewise, a Levite also saw him and passed by on the other side.

But a Samaritan, traveling along the same road, saw the man and took pity on him. He went to him, bandaged his wounds, poured on oil and wine, placed him on his donkey, brought him to an inn, and cared for him. The next day, he took out two denarii and gave them to the innkeeper, asking him to look after the man and promising to reimburse any extra expenses on his return.

Imagine the injured man, vulnerable and abandoned, being helped by someone considered an enemy. The Samaritan's compassion transcended cultural and ethnic boundaries, demonstrating genuine love and kindness. This parable teaches us that we should show love and mercy to everyone, regardless of their background or status.

Lord, help me to embrace Your nurturing love and reflect it in my daily actions. Teach me to be kind, patient, and forgiving, showing Your love to everyone I encounter. Amen.

Key Takeaways:

- Showing God's love in daily actions has a significant impact.
- Acts of kindness and patience mirror God's love to others.
- Stories like the Good Samaritan inspire us to embody God's love.

Bible Study Questions:

1. How does Romans 12:2 guide us in living out God's love?

_____

_____

_____

_____

2. What are practical ways to demonstrate the qualities mentioned in Colossians?

_____

_____

_____

_____

3. How does the Good Samaritan's story challenge us to show God's love?

_____

_____

_____

4. What daily practices can help us fully live out God's love?

_____

_____

_____

_____

5. How can we share God's love with our community?

_____

_____

_____

_____

Journaling Prompts:

1. Reflect on a time when you felt God's love in a special way. How did it transform your view of His care?

_____

_____

_____

_____

_____

_____

_____

_____

_____

_____

_____

2. Write about an area of your life where you need to show God's love. How can you invite His presence?

_____

_____

_____

_____

_____

_____

_____

_____

_____

3. Describe a moment when you felt God's love through someone's kindness. How did it affect your faith and relationships?

_____

_____

_____

_____

_____

_____

_____

_____

_____

_____

4. List ways to show God's love to those around you. How can you reflect His love daily?

_____

_____

_____

_____

_____

_____

_____

_____

_____

_____

5. Identify someone who needs to feel God's love. How can you help share that love with them?

_____

_____

_____

_____

_____

_____

_____

_____

_____

_____

For God so loved the world, that he gave his only begotten Son, that whosoever believeth in him should not perish, but have everlasting life.

John 3:16 KJV

Your word is a lamp to my feet and a light to my path.

Psalms 119:105

Chapter 7: God as Our Guide

Introduction:

Making decisions can be challenging, but knowing God is our guide provides clarity and direction. God offers wisdom through the Bible and the Holy Spirit, leading us on the right path. Trusting God as our guide is like having a reliable friend who knows the way and helps us navigate life's complexities.

Discussion:

Knowing that God is our guide brings direction and clarity in a world filled with uncertainty. Many face difficult decisions and uncertain futures, but trusting God's guidance offers peace and confidence. For example, someone unsure about their career path might find comfort in knowing God is leading them.

God's guidance is like a light in the darkness, illuminating the way. When we need to make decisions or are unsure of our direction, we can

Proverbs 3:5-6 (CSB):
"Trust in the Lord with all your heart and do not rely on your own understanding; in all your ways know him, and he will make your paths straight."

Psalm 119:105 (CSB):
"Your word is a lamp for my feet and a light on my path."

Isaiah 30:21 (CSB): "And whenever you turn to the right or to the left, your ears will hear this command behind you: 'This is the way. Walk in it.'"

turn to prayer and the Bible for guidance. God promises to lead us and help us make the right choices.

Practical Applications:

- Seek God's guidance through prayer and Scripture.
- Look for signs of God's direction in daily life, trusting He is leading you.

Bible Story: The Journey of the Israelites (Exodus 13:17-22; 40:34-38):

The Israelites were enslaved in Egypt for many years until God delivered them through a series of miraculous events. As they journeyed toward the Promised Land, God did not leave them to find their way alone. Instead, He provided a pillar of cloud by day and fire by night to guide them. These pillars represented God's presence and guidance, ensuring the Israelites traveled the right path and reminding them of His protection.

The journey took 40 years, during which the Israelites faced many challenges and hardships. Yet, throughout their journey, the pillars of cloud and fire never left them, demonstrating God's constant care and direction. Even in the wilderness, God's presence was a guiding light, leading them safely to the Promised Land.

Imagine walking through a vast desert without modern navigation tools yet having a divine pillar to guide you. The Israelites' experience teaches us that God's guidance is always available, directing our steps and ensuring we reach our destination safely.

Heavenly Father, thank You for being my guide. Help me to trust in Your wisdom and follow Your path. Give me the clarity to make decisions that honor You and lead me closer to Your purpose for my life. Amen.

Key Takeaways:

- Trusting in God's guidance provides clarity in uncertain times.
- Scriptures like Proverbs 3:5-6 remind us to seek and trust God's guidance.
- Seeking wisdom through prayer and community support helps us understand God's will.

Bible Study Questions:

1. How does Proverbs 3:5-6 teach us to trust God's guidance?

_____

_____

_____

_____

2. How does Psalm 119 emphasize the role of the Bible in guiding us?

_____

_____

_____

_____

3. How can we hear and follow God's voice as described in Isaiah 30:21?

_____

_____

_____

_____

4. What can we learn from the Israelites' journey about trusting God's guidance?

_____

_____

_____

_____

5. How can we apply God's guidance in our daily lives?

_____

_____

_____

_____

Journaling Prompts:

1. Reflect on when you felt God's guidance in making a decision. How did it strengthen your faith?

_____

_____

_____

_____

_____

_____

_____

_____

_____

_____

_____

2. Write about an area of your life where you need God's guidance. How can you seek
His wisdom?

_____

_____

_____

_____

_____

_____

_____

_____

_____

_____

3. Describe a moment when you felt uncertain about your path. How did God's promises of guidance bring you clarity?

_____

_____

_____

_____

_____

_____

_____

_____

_____

_____

4. List ways to seek God's guidance in your daily decisions. How can you discern His will more clearly?

_____

_____

_____

_____

_____

_____

_____

_____

_____

_____

_____

5. Think of someone who needs God's guidance. How can you support them in seeking His direction?

_____

_____

_____

_____

_____

_____

_____

_____

_____

_____

_____

_____

_____

2 PETER 3:9

Chapter 8: God's Patience

Introduction:

Patience is a divine attribute that showcases God's love and faithfulness toward us. God's patience allows us to grow, repent, and align with His will. This chapter highlights how God patiently waits for us and how we can cultivate patience in our lives, reflecting His character. God's patience is like a parent waiting for their child to learn and grow, understanding that it takes time.

Discussion:

God's patience is a powerful trait that gives us the time to grow and align ourselves with His will. Understanding and reflecting on God's patience can transform our approach to life and relationships, especially in a fast-paced world that often demands immediate results. For example, someone facing a prolonged personal struggle might find solace in knowing that God is patient, giving them the time to grow in faith and overcome their challenges.

2 Peter 3:9 (CSB): "The Lord does not delay his promise, as some understand delay, but is patient with you, not wanting any to perish but all to come to repentance."

Psalm 103:8 (CSB): "The Lord is compassionate and gracious, slow to anger and abounding in faithful love."

Romans 2:4 (CSB): "Or do you despise the riches of his kindness, restraint, and patience, not recognizing that God's kindness is intended to lead you to repentance?"

God's patience reveals His understanding of our struggles and weaknesses, waiting for us to turn to Him and providing countless opportunities to learn and grow. This patience is akin to a parent patiently guiding their child, even when the learning process is slow.

Practical Applications:

- Embrace God's patience by being patient with yourself and others, recognizing that growth takes time.
- Wait on God's timing, trusting His plans are for our good.

Bible Story: Jonah (The Book of Jonah)

Jonah, a prophet, is called by God to go to the city of Nineveh and warn its people of impending destruction due to their wickedness. Instead of obeying, Jonah attempts to flee by boarding a ship headed in the opposite direction. God, showing patience, sends a great storm to stop the ship's journey. Realizing the storm is from God, the sailors throw Jonah overboard at his suggestion, and God provides a great fish to swallow him, saving him from drowning. Jonah spends three days and nights in the fish, repenting and praying to God, who commands the fish to release him.

Given a second chance, Jonah goes to Nineveh and delivers God's message. The people of Nineveh, from the king to the commoners, believe in God, declare a fast, and repent in sackcloth and ashes. Seeing their genuine repentance, God relents from the planned destruction. However, Jonah is displeased with God's mercy and goes outside the city to watch what will happen. God uses a plant to teach Jonah about compassion, causing it to grow and provide shade for Jonah, then allowing it to wither the next day. When Jonah expresses anger over the plant's death, God points out Jonah's concern for the plant versus His concern for the people of Nineveh.

Patient Father, I thank You for Your enduring patience with me. Help me to reflect on Your patience in my life, understanding that growth takes time. Teach me to be patient with others, extending the grace that You have shown me. Amen.

Key Takeaways:

• Trusting in God's patience provides peace and assurance.

• Reflecting on verses like 2 Peter 3:9 helps us understand the importance of patience.

• Practicing patience demonstrates our trust in God's perfect timing.

Bible Study Questions:

1. How does 2 Peter 3:9 reflect God's patience toward humanity?

_____

_____

_____

2. What does Psalm 103:8 teach us about the nature of God's patience?

_____

_____

_____

_____

3. How does Romans 2:4 connect God's patience with His kindness and our repentance?

_____

_____

_____

_____

4. What lessons can we learn from the story of Jonah about God's patience?

_____

_____

_____

_____

5. How can we cultivate patience in our own lives, mirroring God's patience?

_____

_____

_____

_____

Journaling Prompts:

1. Reflect on a time when you experienced God's patience. How did it change your view of His love and grace?

_____

_____

_____

_____

_____

_____

_____

_____

_____

2. Write about an area in your life where you need to develop patience. How can you seek God's help to grow in patience?

_____

_____

_____

_____

_____

_____

_____

_____

_____

_____

_____

3. Describe a moment when you felt impatient or frustrated. How did reflecting on God's patience bring you peace?

_____

_____

_____

_____

_____

_____

_____

_____

_____

_____

_____

4. List ways to practice patience in your daily life. How can you embody God's patience?

_____

_____

_____

_____

_____

_____

_____

_____

_____

_____

5. Identify someone who needs patience. How can you support them and model God's patience in your interactions?

_____

_____

_____

_____

_____

_____

_____

_____

_____

Fatherly Attributes

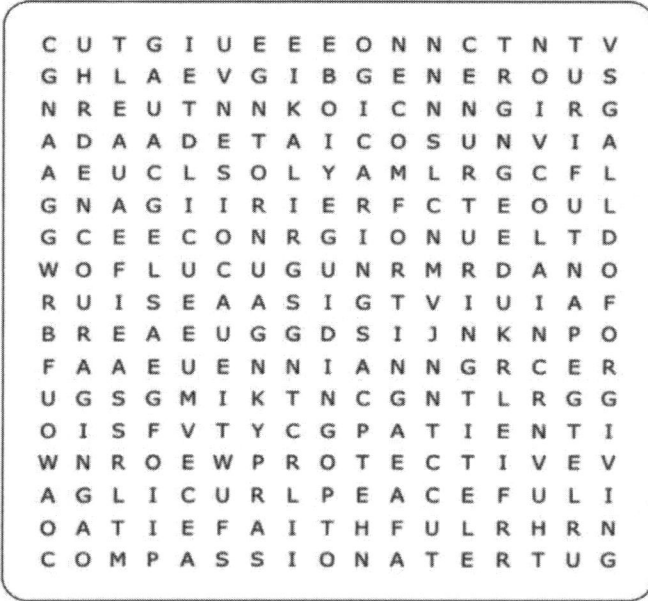

```
C U T G I U E E E O N N C T N T V
G H L A E V G I B G E N E R O U S
N R E U T N N K O I C N N G I R G
A D A A D E T A I C O S U N V I A
A E U C L S O L Y A M L R G C F L
G N A G I I R I E R F C T E O U L
G C E E C O N R G I O N U E L T D
W O F L U C U G U N R M R D A N O
R U I S E A A S I G T V I U I A F
B R E A E U G G D S I J N K N P O
F A A E U E N N I A N N G R C E R
U G S G M I K T N C G N T L R G G
O I S F V T Y C G P A T I E N T I
W N R O E W P R O T E C T I V E V
A G L I C U R L P E A C E F U L I
O A T I E F A I T H F U L R H R N
C O M P A S S I O N A T E R T U G
```

Solution on page 117

Caring	Comforting	Compassionate
Encouraging	Faithful	Forgiving
Generous	Gentle	Gracious
Guiding	Healing	Kind
Loving	Nurturing	Patient
Peaceful	Protective	Wise

As we conclude this journey through understanding God's comforting presence, provision, protection, healing, and patient love, I pray that you have found solace and inspiration in these truths. Embracing these aspects of God's character allows us to live more fulfilled lives, reflecting His love and grace in our actions.

May you continue to grow in faith, trusting God's guidance and embodying His love in your relationships and daily life. As you seek His comfort, provision, protection, healing, and patience, may you experience His blessings and share His love with those around you.

Dear Lord, thank You for being our comforter, provider, protector, healer, and guide. Help us to embody Your love and patience in our lives, reflecting Your grace to all we meet. May we grow in faith and trust in Your perfect plan for us. In Jesus' name, Amen.

Bonus Material

Group Study Guide

Week 1: God as Our Comforter

Discussion Questions:

1) How have you experienced God's comfort in your life?

_____

_____

_____

What scriptures bring you the most comfort during difficult times?

_____

_____

_____

2) How can you offer God's comfort to others?

_____

_____

_____

3) In what ways can the group support each other in seeking God's comfort?

_____

_____

_____

4) How does understanding God's role as a Comforter impact your daily life?

_____

_____

_____

Activity: Write a letter of encouragement to someone who needs comfort, using scripture to support your words. Share your letters with the group and discuss the impact of offering comfort through words.

Activity 2: Create a "Comfort Care Package" for someone in need, including items like an encouraging book, comforting scriptures, and a personal note. Deliver it as a group and reflect on the experience

Write a short prayer of thanks:

_____

_____

_____

_____

Week 2: God as Our Provider

Discussion Questions:

1) Share a time when you experienced God's provision in an unexpected way.

_____

_____

_____

2) How does trusting in God's provision impact your daily life?

_____

_____

_____

3) How can you be a vessel of God's provision for others?

_____

_____

_____

4) What are some practical steps to increase our faith in God's provision?

_____

_____

_____

5) How can gratitude for God's provision change our perspective?

_____

_____

_____

Activity: Organize a group service project to help meet a need in your community. Reflect on how this act of service helps you understand God's provision better and discuss the experiences with the group.

Activity 2: Create a "Blessing Jar" where group members can write down instances of God's provision they experience throughout the week. Share these blessings at the next meeting to encourage one another.

What would you add to your blessing jar?

_____

_____

_____

_____

_____

Week 3: God as Our Protector

Discussion Questions:

1) Discuss a situation where you felt God's protection.

_____

_____

_____

_____

2) What are your favorite scriptures about God's protection?

_____

_____

_____

_____

3) How can we pray for God's protection over our families and communities?

_____

_____

_____

_____

4) How do we balance trust in God's protection with taking responsible actions for safety?

_____

_____

_____

5) How can understanding God's protection help reduce anxiety and fear?

_____

_____

_____

Activity: Create a prayer wall where group members can post prayer requests for protection. Spend time each week praying over these requests and share any updates or answered prayers.

Activity 2: Plan a safety awareness day in your community, incorporating prayer and practical safety tips. Discuss how physical safety and spiritual protection intersect.

Notes:

_____

_____

_____

_____

_____

_____

_____

_____

Week 4: God as Our Healer

Discussion Questions:

1) Share a testimony of healing in your life or someone you know.

_____

_____

_____

_____

_____

2) How can we build our faith in God's healing power?

_____

_____

_____

_____

3) What practical steps can we take to seek God's healing?

_____

_____

_____

_____

4) How can we support others who are seeking healing?

_____

_____

_____

5) How does God's healing encompass physical, emotional, and spiritual aspects?

_____

_____

_____

_____

Activity: Spend time in prayer for those in need of healing, anointing with oil as led by the Spirit. Discuss the significance of anointing and share any experiences of healing.

Activity 2: Host a healing service or prayer night, inviting those in need of healing to come for prayer and support. Share testimonies of healing and encourage faith in God's power to heal.

Who can I pray for this week?

_____

_____

_____

_____

_____

Week 5: God as Our Loving Father

Discussion Questions:

1) How does understanding God as a loving Father change your view of yourself?

_____

_____

_____

_____

2) What does it mean to live as a beloved child of God?

_____

_____

_____

_____

3) How can we reflect God's fatherly love to others?

_____

_____

_____

_____

4) In what ways can we deepen our relationship with God as our Father?

_____

_____

_____

_____

5) How can we help others understand and experience God's fatherly love?

_____

_____

_____

_____

Activity: Write a personal letter to God, expressing your gratitude for His fatherly love and care. Share your letters with the group if you feel comfortable, and discuss how this exercise has impacted your understanding of God's love.

Activity 2: Plan a "Father's Love" retreat where the group can spend extended time in prayer, worship, and reflection on God's fatherly love. Include activities like group discussions, personal reflection time, and worship sessions.

Notes:

_____

_____

_____

_____

_____

_____

Week 6: Embracing God's Nurturing Love in Daily Life

Discussion Questions:

1) How can you make a conscious effort to show God's love in your daily interactions?

_____

_____

_____

_____

2) What are some specific ways you can demonstrate kindness, patience, and forgiveness?

_____

_____

_____

_____

3) How does focusing on God's love help you respond to challenging situations?

_____

_____

_____

4) How do acts of kindness and patience reflect God's love to others?

_____

_____

_____

5) What steps can we take to consistently embody God's love in our relationships?

_____

_____

_____

_____

Activity: Plan and execute a random acts of kindness challenge as a group. Share your experiences and reflections on how these acts impacted you and others.

Activity 2: Develop a "30-Day Love Challenge" where each group member commits to performing a specific act of kindness or love each day. Share progress and reflections weekly.

Week 7: God as Our Guide

Discussion Questions:

1) How has God guided you through difficult decisions in your life?

_____

_____

_____

_____

2) What are some ways to seek God's guidance in everyday situations?

_____

_____

_____

3) How does knowing God is your guide bring you peace and confidence?

_____

_____

_____

4) What scriptures help you trust in God's guidance?

_____

_____

_____

5) How can you encourage others to seek God's guidance?

_____

_____

_____

Activity: Create a "Guidance Journal" where each group member writes about times when they felt guided by God. Share entries with the group and discuss how recognizing God's guidance has strengthened your faith.

Activity 2: Plan a group outing where you take turns leading and guiding each other to a specific destination. Reflect on the experience and how it relates to following God's guidance in life.

Guidance Journal Entry:

_____

_____

_____

_____

_____

_____

Week 8: God's Patience

Discussion Questions:

1) Reflect on a time when you experienced God's patience. How did it affect you?

_____

_____

_____

_____

2) How can understanding God's patience help you be more patient with others?

_____

_____

_____

3) What areas of your life require more patience?

_____

_____

_____

_____

4) How can you invite God into those areas?

_____

_____

_____

5) How does God's patience reflect His love and care for us?

_____

_____

_____

6) How can we demonstrate patience in our daily interactions?

_____

_____

_____

_____

Activity: Practice patience as a group by participating in an activity that requires waiting, such as planting seeds and watching them grow over time. Discuss the parallels between this process and experiencing God's patience in our lives.

Activity 2: Develop a "Patience Project" where each member commits to practicing patience in a specific area of their life for a month. Share progress and reflections on how this practice has impacted your relationship with God and other.

The Prodigal Son

```
T E I C O M P A S S I O N T T E E Y
T F A T H E R K H F L C O T U F R O
F G U O C F E A S T G C C U Y T S H
E R L D H E S E S L H A C C N N E R
R A R D T A L E E N O R S U O A H E
F T I Y E T O E R H C V O L T O R C
N I E S J I R S B S C C E R E O F O
J T P O V E R T Y R D R E R D T S N
E U M E O L D E R O A G A R I O E C
A D E K O S E G F R N T E L E P R I
L E I R V C L O O U O R I H D W W L
O E R A A I O U O A R R I O Y A B I
U V Z R N O L Y Q E U A E R N S T A
S S B W S S R E C K L E S S Y T E T
Y M E O I I N H E R I T A N C E Y I
E H E R C T R T E D N E O N T F U O
I A L K Q F A R E T U R N G I U R N
F O R G I V E N E S S S O E A L Q T
```

Solution on page 118

Celebration	Compassion	Country
Embrace	Far	Father
Feast	Forgiveness	Gratitude
Inheritance	Jealousy	Love
Older	Poverty	Reckless
Reconciliation	Return	Wasteful
Work	Younger	

Daily Devotional Plan

A structured devotional plan can keep you focused and help you grow your faith. <u>Look up your daily verse. Read it. Highlight it. Write it.</u> Throughout the day, dwell on the Scripture of the day.

Here's a 30-day plan to guide you:

Week 1: God's Comfort

Day 1: ***Psalm 34:18*** – Reflect on how God is near to the brokenhearted.

Day 2: ***Isaiah 41:10*** – Meditate on God's promise to uphold you.

Day 3: ***John 14:1-3*** – Consider Jesus' assurance of preparing a place for you.

Day 4: ***Matthew 11:28-30*** – Rest in Jesus' invitation to find rest in Him.

Day 5: ***2 Corinthians 1:3-4*** – Think about how you can comfort others with the comfort you've received.

Day 6: ***Psalm 23:4*** – Reflect on God's presence even in the darkest valleys.

Day 7: **Reflection and Prayer** – Spend time journaling and praying about God's comfort in your life.

Week 2: God's Provision

Day 8: ***Philippians 4:19*** – Reflect on God's promise to supply all your needs.

Day 9: ***Matthew 6:26-34*** – Consider how God provides for the birds and flowers.

Day 10: ***Psalm 37:25*** – Reflect on God's faithfulness through the years.

Day 11: ***2 Corinthians 9:8*** – Think about how God makes grace abound to you.

Day 12: ***Genesis 22:14*** – Remember God's provision for Abraham and how He provides for you.

Day 13: ***Deuteronomy 2:7*** – Reflect on God's care during times of wandering.

Day 14: **Reflection and Prayer** – Spend time journaling and praying about God's provision in your life.

Week 3: God's Protection

Day 15: ***Psalm 91:1-4*** – Reflect on finding refuge under God's wings.

Day 16: ***Psalm 121:7-8*** – Consider how God protects your coming and going.

Day 17: ***2 Samuel 22:3-4*** – Reflect on God as your shield and stronghold.

Day 18: ***Isaiah 54:17*** – Meditate on God's promise that no weapon formed against you will prosper.

Day 19: ***2 Thessalonians 3:3*** – Think about how God strengthens and protects you from the evil one.

Day 20: ***Proverbs 18:10*** – Reflect on the name of the Lord as a strong tower.

Day 21: **Reflection and Prayer** – Spend time journaling and praying about God's protection in your life.

Week 4: God's Healing

Day 22: ***James 5:14-15*** – Reflect on the power of prayer and anointing for healing.

Day 23: ***Psalm 103:2-3*** – Consider God's benefits, including healing all your diseases.

Day 24: ***Isaiah 53:5*** – Meditate on the healing brought by Jesus' wounds.

Day 25: ***Exodus 15:26*** – Reflect on God as your healer.

Day 26: ***Jeremiah 17:14*** – Pray for God's healing in your life.

Day 27: ***3 John 1:2*** – Reflect on God's desire for you to prosper and be in good health.

Day 28: **Reflection and Prayer** – Spend time journaling and praying about God's healing in your life.

Week 5: God's Fatherly Love

Day 29: **Romans 8:15** – Reflect on your adoption as God's child and calling Him "Abba, Father."

Day 30: **1 John 3:1** – Consider the great love the Father has lavished on you, calling you His child.

```
W N U E H R L R A O R E F U G E S E
M T S N N A H P R O V I S I O N E E
A F A A I S S R E N M C L C O E R R
U O M T J R L T H A E H O O R E O A
T R A P E T A P I C L I V E R T I H
H G R N D X R H A L H I E A C N S N
I I I L T A B R A H A M N E L F F U
W V T R O E G G E G S A T G N N A S
H E A D A N I E L A F O O S O F I W
A N N S R U S I N I R G T I A B T C
G E O H I T N U N P C E S I E T H P
A S H P R O M I S E S S O T U R F R
R S T V R E F S L H A R R L G U U O
E F A T H E R L Y P E O C A N S L D
E A P O R F T I M A F E E N L T K I
N O L E R O E M M G D P H A T H G
X F D V A V C H O O H E A L E R S A
D N L J E H I C N U R T U R I N G L
```

Solution on page 117

Abraham	Comfort	Compassion
Daniel	Faithful	Fatherly
Forgiveness	Grace	Hagar
Healer	Healing	Love
Nurturing	Prodigal	Promises
Protector	Provision	Refuge
Samaritan	Trust	

Q&A Section

Question 1: How can I feel God's presence more in my daily life?

Answer: Feeling God's presence can be cultivated through regular prayer, reading the Bible, and practicing gratitude. Set aside time each day to pray and read Scripture, inviting God into every aspect of your life. Journaling your thoughts and experiences can also help you recognize His presence more clearly. Additionally, seek to be mindful and present in your daily activities, looking for God's hand in the mundane and the extraordinary moments.

Question 2: What should I do when it seems God is not providing for my needs?

Answer: During times of feeling you have not enough, it's essential to continue trusting in God's faithfulness. Reflect on past instances where God provided for you and others. Pray for patience and wisdom to see how God might work in ways you don't yet understand. Seek support from your faith community, and remember Philippians 4:19: "And my God will supply all your needs according to his riches in glory in Christ Jesus." Also, consider if there are areas where God might be teaching you to rely on Him more fully or prompting you to take specific actions.

Question 3: How can I better understand God's will for my life?

Answer: Understanding God's will involves seeking Him through prayer, Scripture, and wise counsel. Proverbs 3:5-6 encourages us to trust the Lord with all our heart and not rely on our understanding. God often reveals His will through His Word, the guidance of the Holy Spirit, and the advice of trusted mentors and friends. Additionally, pay attention to the desires and passions God has placed in your heart, as these can often align with His plans for you. Remember to be patient; understanding God's will is a journey that unfolds over time.

Question 4: How can I strengthen my faith in God's healing power?

Answer: Strengthening your faith in God's healing power involves immersing yourself in Scripture, prayer, and testimonies of healing. Reflect on verses like James 5:14-15 and Isaiah 53:5. Attend healing services or prayer groups and witness how God works through others. Maintain an attitude of gratitude and expectancy, believing that God is able and willing to heal. Surround yourself with a community of believers who can pray for and encourage you in your faith journey.

Question 5: How can I maintain a strong faith during challenging times?

Answer: Maintaining a strong faith during challenging times involves staying rooted in God's Word and prayer. Regularly remind yourself of God's promises and His past faithfulness. Surround yourself with a supportive faith community to encourage and pray for you. Keep a journal to document your struggles and how God is working through them, which can be a source of encouragement. Engage in worship and praise, focusing on God's greatness rather than your circumstances.

Question 6: How do I overcome feelings of doubt and fear?

Answer: Overcoming feelings of doubt and fear starts with recognizing that they are natural emotions but do not have to control you. Turn to scriptures that speak about God's peace and strength, such as Isaiah 41:10 and Philippians 4:6-7. Pray for God's help overcoming these feelings, and be honest with Him about your struggles. Surround yourself with positive influences and people who can uplift you. Practice gratitude and focus on the blessings in your life, which can shift your perspective from fear to faith.

Question 7: How can I grow in my relationship with God?

Answer: Growing in your relationship with God involves spending regular time in prayer and reading the Bible. Seek to know God more deeply through His Word and listen to His voice. Engage in worship and participate in a faith community where you can learn and grow together. Serve others and look for ways to demonstrate God's love in practical ways. Continually seek to align your life with God's will and be open to His leading.

LOVE GOD

LOVE PEOPLE

Additional Bible Study Questions

God as Our Comforter

1. How does God's promise to be near the brokenhearted (Psalm 34:18) provide you with comfort in your current situation?

_____

_____

_____

_____

2. In what ways can you actively seek God's comfort during times of stress or sorrow?

_____

_____

_____

_____

3. How can understanding God's comfort change your perspective on suffering?

_____

_____

_____

_____

4. What practical ways can you share God's comfort with those around you?

_____

_____

_____

_____

God as Our Provider

1. Reflect on a time when you doubted God's provision. How did He eventually meet your needs?

    _____

    _____

    _____

    _____

2. How does Jesus' teaching in Matthew 6:26-34 encourage you to trust in God's provision?

    _____

    _____

    _____

    _____

3. What areas of your life do you need to trust God more fully for provision?

    _____

    _____

    _____

    _____

4. How can you cultivate a heart of gratitude for God's daily provision?

_____

_____

_____

_____

God as Our Protector

1. How does knowing that God is your protector influence your response to fear and anxiety?

_____

_____

_____

_____

2. What can you learn from the story of Daniel in the lions' den about trusting God's protection?

_____

_____

_____

_____

3. How can you remind yourself of God's protection in everyday situations?

_____

_____

_____

4. How does Psalm 91:4 inspire you to seek refuge in God?

_____

_____

_____

_____

God as Our Healer

1. How does the story of Jesus healing the blind man (John 9:1-12) illustrate His power and compassion?

_____

_____

_____

_____

2. What steps can you take to seek God's healing in areas of your life that need restoration?

_____

_____

_____

_____

3. How can you support and pray for others who are seeking healing?

_____

_____

_____

4. Reflect on how God's healing encompasses physical, emotional, and spiritual aspects.

_____

_____

_____

_____

God as Our Loving Father

1. How does the parable of the Prodigal Son (Luke 15:11-32) shape your understanding of God's fatherly love?

_____

_____

_____

_____

2. In what ways can you embrace your identity as a beloved child of God?

_____

_____

_____

_____

3. How can you reflect God's fatherly love in your interactions with others?

_____

_____

4. What does it mean to you to call God "Abba, Father" (Romans 8:15)?

_____

_____

_____

_____

Embracing God's Nurturing Love in Daily Life

1. How can you make a conscious effort to show God's love in your daily interactions?

_____

_____

_____

_____

2. What are some specific ways you can demonstrate kindness and patience in challenging situations?

_____

_____

_____

_____

3. How does focusing on God's love help you deal with difficult people or circumstances?

_____

_____

_____

_____

4. Reflect on how simple acts of love and kindness can impact others and glorify God.

_____

_____

_____

_____

God as Our Guide

1. How has God guided you through difficult decisions in your life?

_____

_____

_____

_____

2. How does knowing God is your guide bring you peace and confidence?

_____

_____

_____

_____

3. What scriptures help you trust in God's guidance?

_____

_____

_____

_____

_____

4.   How do you discern God's voice from other influences?

_____

_____

_____

_____

God's Patience

1.   How can understanding God's patience help you be more patient with others?

_____

_____

_____

_____

2.   What areas of your life require more patience? How can you invite God into those areas?

_____

_____

_____

_____

3. How does God's patience reflect His love and care for us?

_____

_____

_____

_____

4. How can we demonstrate patience in our daily interactions?

_____

_____

_____

_____

Journal Prompts

God as Our Comforter

1. Write about a time when you felt God's comfort during a difficult situation. How did it change your outlook on the situation?

_____

_____

_____

_____

_____

_____

_____

_____

_____

2. Reflect on the ways God has used others to bring comfort to you. How can you pass that on to someone else?

_____

_____

_____

_____

_____

_____

_____

_____

_____

_____

_____

_____

_____

_____

3. Consider a current challenge you are facing. How can you invite God's
    comforting presence into this situation?

_____

_____

_____

_____

_____

_____

_____

_____

_____

_____

_____

_____

God as Our Provider

1. Reflect on a moment when you were worried about provision but saw God come through. How did it strengthen your faith?

_____

_____

_____

_____

_____

_____

_____

_____

_____

_____

_____

2. List some ways God has provided for you in the past week. How can you cultivate gratitude for these blessings?

_____

_____

_____

_____

_____

_____

_____

_____

_____

_____

_____

3. Think about an area where you are struggling to trust God for provision. Write a prayer asking for His help and guidance.

_____

_____

_____

_____

_____

_____

_____

_____

_____

_____

_____

_____

God as Our Protector

1. Describe when you felt God's protection over you or your loved ones. How
   did it impact your faith?

_____

_____

_____

_____

_____

_____

_____

_____

_____

_____

_____

_____

2. Write about any fears or anxieties you are currently facing. How can you trust God's protection in these areas?

_____

_____

_____

_____

_____

_____

_____

_____

_____

_____

_____

_____

_____

3. Reflect on Psalm 91 and what it means for you. How can you apply this
    Scripture to your life?

_____

_____

_____

_____

_____

_____

_____

_____

_____

_____

_____

God as Our Healer

1. Write about a time when you experienced God's healing, whether physically, emotionally, or spiritually. How did it affect your relationship with Him?

_____

_____

_____

_____

_____

_____

_____

_____

_____

_____

2. Reflect on areas of your life that need healing. How can you seek God's restoration in these areas?

_____

_____

_____

_____

_____

_____

_____

_____

_____

_____

_____

3. Consider someone you know who needs healing. Write a prayer for them and think about ways you can support them.

_____

_____

_____

_____

_____

_____

_____

_____

_____

_____

_____

_____

_____

_____

God as Our Loving Father

1. Reflect on how understanding God as your loving Father has changed your view of yourself and your life.

_____

_____

_____

_____

_____

_____

_____

_____

_____

_____

_____

_____

2. Write about an experience where you profoundly felt God's fatherly love.
    How did it impact you?

_____

_____

_____

_____

_____

_____

_____

_____

_____

_____

_____

_____

3. Think about how you can show God's fatherly love to others. Write down some practical steps you can take.

_____

_____

_____

_____

_____

_____

_____

_____

_____

_____

_____

_____

_____

Embracing God's Nurturing Love in Daily Life

1. Write about a recent experience where you showed God's love through your actions. How did it affect you and others involved?

_____

_____

_____

_____

_____

_____

_____

_____

_____

_____

_____

_____

_____

2. Reflect on how you can incorporate acts of kindness and patience into your daily routine. What are some specific actions you can take?

_____

_____

_____

_____

_____

_____

_____

_____

_____

_____

_____

_____

3. Consider how embracing God's love has transformed your relationships.
    Write about these changes and how they have impacted your life.

_____

_____

_____

_____

_____

_____

_____

_____

_____

_____

_____

God as Our Guide

1. Reflect on a recent decision you had to make. How did you seek God's guidance in that situation?

_____

_____

_____

_____

_____

_____

_____

_____

_____

_____

_____

_____

2. Write about a time when you felt lost or unsure about your path. How did God guide you through that period?

_____

_____

_____

_____

_____

_____

_____

_____

_____

_____

_____

3. List the ways in which you hear God's voice in your life. How do you distinguish His guidance from other influences?

_____

_____

_____

_____

_____

_____

_____

_____

_____

_____

_____

_____

God's Patience

1. Reflect on a time when you experienced God's patience. How did it affect you?

_____

_____

_____

_____

_____

_____

_____

_____

_____

_____

_____

_____

2. How can understanding God's patience help you be more patient with others?

_____

_____

_____

_____

_____

_____

_____

_____

_____

_____

_____

3. What areas of your life require more patience? How can you invite God into those areas?

_____

_____

_____

_____

_____

_____

_____

_____

_____

Trust in the LORD

Prayers for Different Situations

Prayer for Comfort

Heavenly Father, I come to You feeling overwhelmed and in need of Your comforting presence. Help me to feel Your nearness and find peace in Your promises. Surround me with Your love and grace, and guide me through this difficult time. Amen.

Prayer for Provision

Dear Lord, I trust in Your provision for all my needs. Help me to rely on You and not be anxious about tomorrow. Provide for me and my family in ways that bring glory to Your name. Thank You for Your faithfulness and generosity. Amen.

Prayer for Protection

Gracious God, I seek Your protection over my life and the lives of my loved ones. Shield us from harm and guide us through the challenges we face. Help us to trust in Your mighty power and find refuge under Your wings. Amen.

Prayer for Healing

Loving Father, I ask for Your healing touch on my body, mind, and spirit. Restore me to health and renew my strength. Help me to trust in Your power to heal and to find peace in Your presence. Thank You for Your love and care. Amen.

Prayer for Fatherly Love

Abba, Father, thank You for loving me unconditionally and calling me Your child. Help me to embrace Your fatherly love and live confidently in Your care. Guide me to reflect Your love to others and to grow deeper in my relationship with You. Amen.

Prayer for Guidance

Heavenly Father, I seek Your wisdom and guidance in all my decisions. Lead me on the right path and help me to discern Your will for my life. Give me clarity and peace as I follow Your direction. Surround me with wise counsel and help me to trust in Your plans. Thank You for being my guide and shepherd. Amen.

Now, take a moment to reflect on what you've learned and how you can apply it in your life. Consider writing down your thoughts, setting goals, and praying for God's guidance as you move forward. Share these insights with others and encourage them to explore the depths of God's love and care.

About the Author

Hope Beasley is a stay-at-home wife and mom from Mobile, Alabama. At the age of 36, she graduated from the University of South Alabama with a bachelor's degree in Psychology, intending to become a Domestic Violence counselor. However, what began as a temporary position turned into a 15-year career as a Book Buyer at Choice Books of Gulf States, a Christian book distributor.

Hope is passionate about Autism awareness, women's issues, the power of God's forgiveness, and the power of prayer. She has previously published three ebooks and is excited to share her latest book, a Bible study titled Embracing Our Father's Love: A Journey of Faith and Healing. Through this book, she hopes to open readers' eyes and hearts to God's incredible love, especially for those who lack a relationship with their earthly father.

Solution pg 28

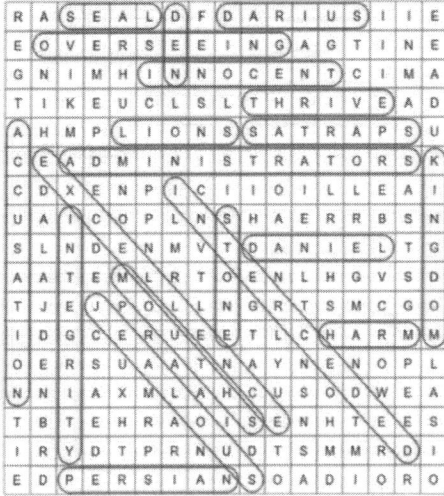

Solution pg 36

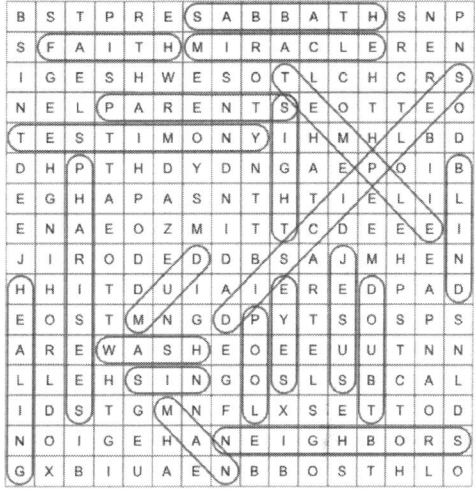

Solution pg 65

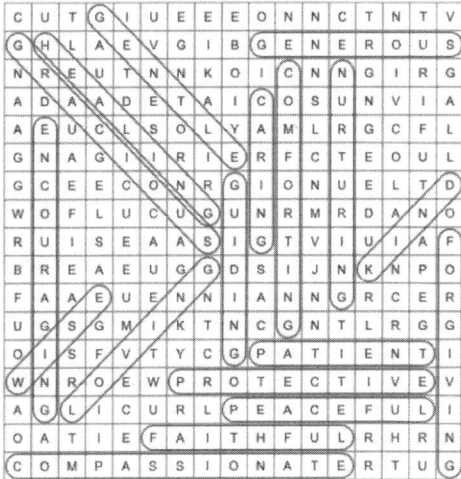

Solution pg 83

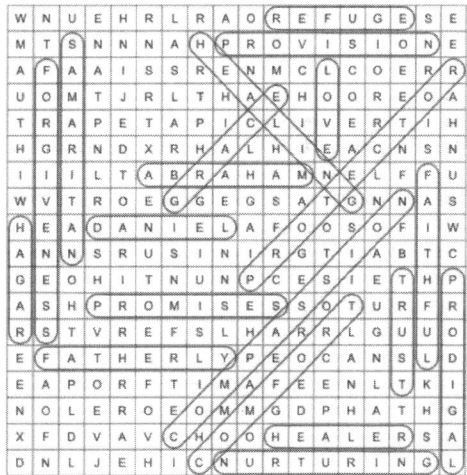

```
T  E  I  C  O  M  P  A  S  S  I  O  N  T  T  E  E  Y
T  F  A  T  H  E  R  K  H  F  L  C  O  T  U  F  R  O
F  G  U  O  C  F  E  A  S  T  G  C  C  U  Y  T  S  H
E  R  L  D  H  E  S  E  S  L  H  A  C  C  N  N  E  R
R  A  R  D  T  A  L  E  E  N  O  R  S  U  O  A  H  E
F  T  I  Y  E  T  O  E  R  H  C  V  O  L  T  O  R  C
N  I  E  S  J  I  R  S  B  S  C  C  E  R  E  O  F  O
J  T  P  O  V  E  R  T  Y  R  D  R  E  R  D  T  S  N
E  U  M  E  O  L  D  E  R  O  A  G  A  R  I  O  E  C
A  D  E  K  O  S  E  G  F  R  N  T  E  L  E  P  R  I
L  E  I  R  V  C  L  O  O  U  O  R  I  H  D  W  W  L
O  E  R  A  A  I  O  U  O  A  R  R  I  O  Y  A  B  I
U  V  Z  R  N  O  L  Y  Q  E  U  A  E  R  N  S  T  A
S  S  B  W  S  S  R  E  C  K  L  E  S  S  Y  T  E  T
Y  M  E  O  I  I  N  H  E  R  I  T  A  N  C  E  Y  I
E  H  E  R  C  T  R  T  E  D  N  E  O  N  T  F  U  O
I  A  L  K  Q  F  A  R  E  T  U  R  N  G  I  U  R  N
F  O  R  G  I  V  E  N  E  S  S  S  O  E  A  L  Q  T
```

FOR SPECIAL
notes

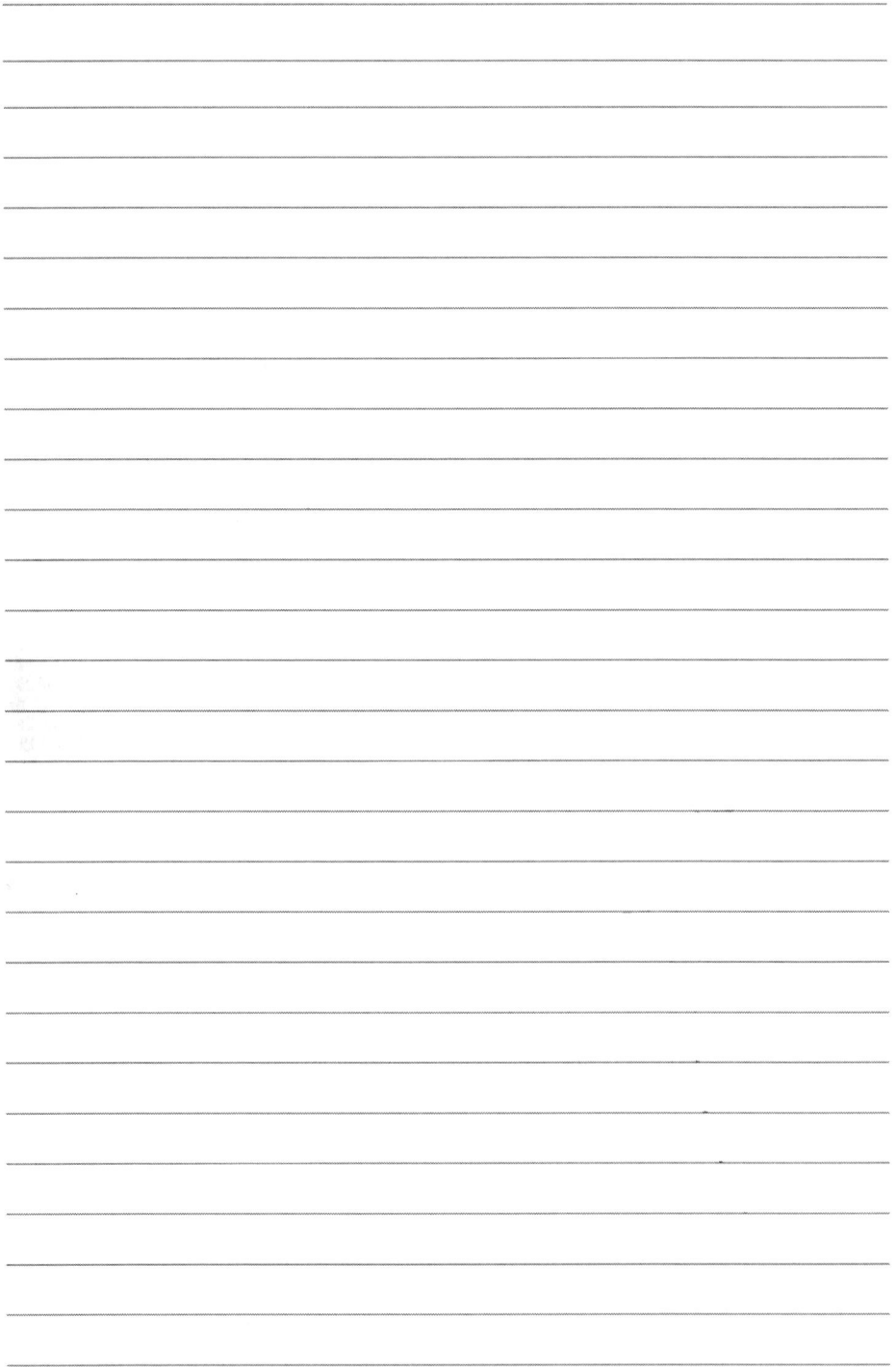

Made in the USA
Monee, IL
04 November 2024

69319967R00068